POETRY NOW

MIDLANDS

1992

First published in Great Britain in 1992 by
POETRY NOW
4 Hythegate, Werrington,
Peterborough, PE4 7ZP

Foreword

Although we are a nation of poetry writers we are accused of not reading poetry and not buying poetry books: after many years of listening to the incessant gripes of poetry publishers, I can only assume that the books they publish, in general, are books that most people do not want to read.

Poetry should not be obscure, introverted, and as cryptic as a crossword puzzle: it is the poet's duty to reach out and embrace the world.

The world owes the poet nothing and we should not be expected to dig and delve into a rambling discourse searching for some inner meaning.

The reason we write poetry (and almost all of us do) is because we want to communicate: an ideal; an idea; or a specific feeling. Poetry is as essential in communication, as a letter; a radio; a telephone, and the main criteria for selecting the poems in this anthology is very simple: they communicate.

Faced with hundreds of poems and a limited amount of space the task of choosing the final poems is difficult and as editor one has to try to be as detached as possible - quite often editors can become a barrier in the writer - reader exchange - acting as go between, making the connection, not censoring because of personal taste.

In this volume around one hundred and four poems are presented to the reader for their enjoyment. The subject matter is as varied as the writers themselves, love, hate, war, peace, the seasons, etc.

The poetry is written on all levels; the simple and the complex both having their own appeal.

The success of this collection, and all previous Poetry Now anthologies, relies on the fact that there are as many individual readers as there are writers, and in the diversity of styles, subjects, and forms there really is something to please, excite, and hopefully, inspire everyone who reads the book.

This is a book that is a representative collection of poetry as it is being written today: Poetry Now.

Contents

If I Were Not Me Who Would I Be?

One speck of time we have predestined,
and though the when and wherefore are as obscure
as the moment next to now
and the distance to our goal immeasurable,
our future is assured.
We may hide and shrink away
or laugh and show contempt,
but that time will come,
and we shall see that the tangled skein of lives
that cross and thread our own
are as blossom strewn across the direct path
that spans from birth to death.

Though I pass through winds that blow through me,
or as cold bones
lie entombed by wet and airless earth,
still I will see and touch and be,
for the spirit soul - the aura -
cannot be chained and locked in time
or held by logic;
and if some time I ride the raven's wing,
melt to the inside of a leaf,
or from some distant space
survey the dark side of the moon,
then the future and the past will be as one
and the present when I touch you as I pass.

Jeremy Duffield

Mirages

Blue smoke curling upwards
Lazy spiralling slow-motion vision
Half-seen shapes distorted by mist
Twisting round in the brain
Blurring the crisp clarity of youth.
Uncertain pain shatters the easy mind
Parting to float with the air
Round and round in tumbling
Images seen through a hazy glass.
Floating with the wispy smoke
Cirrus in the sky and beneath
The cold dreamers land
Stretching to a far horizon
From where horizon stretches
To horizon's thoughts.
And playing in the valleys
The slumbering smoke gathers
And densely covers the eyes,
And all that was known
Was lost, and seeing gloom
They wait; ash fills the valleys
The deep drawn breath
Breaches the fog with light
And with sudden sight
My cigarette goes out.

P G Cuthill

Peculiar Petunia

Peculiar Petunia
You are such a luscious flower,
Wrapped in pretty petals
For us insects to devour.

O tasty teasing temptress
My ardour cannot halt,
But when I eat your undergrowth
You always cry 'Assault!'

Peculiar Petunia
I'm not a rapist or a killer,
Just a mess of primal instincts
A humble caterpillar.

John Vaites

Out-Foxed

They raised the alarm. Tamed
wildfowl, clustered on my window-
ledges, alerted me, their calls
frenzied, strident, distressed.
Oily eyes in the hedge reflected
my torch beam. I advanced, the
birds followed silent now, wary,
staying behind me.
Stick thrown, eyes vanished.
They surged past me, noisily
triumphant. *They* did it!

Margaret Willoughby

Moonrise Over Charlestown

I watched the moonrise over Charlestown,
Gazing so long on that distant world
It took all the sea in its brightness;
Silver to black, we danced by the quayside,
Lightly the trot over uneven stones,
Rattling the chains of the buoys on the briny,
Bobbing like tenders, lighter and empty.

We never felt the wind or the rain in our faces,
Cracking our skin like looking-glass windows,
We never dropped on the cobbled, cold harbour wall,
Not until Ben came ashore in the lamplight,
The catch all salted with slivers of daybreak,
They were the longest hours ever of mine,
Those ages of fishing and moonlight and brine.

Nicholas Clark

The Wandering Kind

Long years ago, when life was young
I was the wandering kind,
A product of an hungry age
When jobs were hard to find.
I walked the breadth of Britain,
Worked if, and as I could.
But, no place held me captive
For longer than it should.

I dreamt my dreams beneath the stars,
Where I might lay my head,
In field and ditch or hedgerow tall,
In open barn or shed.
I swam the early morning stream
And climbed the misty peak.
I trod forsaken frozen wastes
Till winter touched my cheek.

It took me years to settle down,
For life to unify,
To put an end to wandering
Beneath the restless sky.
And now it is my son that's young
And he's the wandering kind,
A product of an hungry age
Where jobs are hard to find.

Stan Smith

Air Traffic Control

The robin died against the north wall of the Portuguese castle.
Strictly partisan, it entered the air space above Sintra
Without clearance and broke its wing.
An avenging angel touched its flight.

Now the unbruised eye of death fixes its stare on the rising star.
Soft-bellied in the setting sun, the russet feathers flipped
By a keening wind
Give semblance of ill-fated flight.

J M Tomlinson

Ode

There is something
That is even more beautiful
Than a rose, or a lover ...
- That which made them grow -
Life itself.
So there is really
No death ...
Just and end of the image,
There for the moment
To remind us.

Lisa Ammerman

Poppies

The poppies of Flanders are red
For blood and for glory,
But red is for rebellion
And war is all obedience.

The poppies of peace are white
For doves and for denial,
But white is for innocence
And peace is not guiltless.

Where is a poppy as black
As the grave and the hell-mouth?
For black is for mourning
And death is a darkness.

No sale for the poppies
Whilst guns supplant ploughshares.
Not red for rejoicing
Nor white, for clean linen.

Jean M Hayward

The Splendour of Solitude

I stand alone amid the summer fens amid the
greens and golds that sparkle with the morning
dew, dancing to the rhythm of a passing breeze
blowing from the eastern shores.

No other sight can rival the glory of the fields in bloom
growing neath the pastel blue, reaching t'ward the
yellow, arms held high praising these days of
majesty.

And the air hangs heavy, laden with the scent of
freedom, rising from the fertile soil, drifting on
the sultry winds wandering these lovely plains
of England.

Nothing can disturb my heart as I rest upon the
sweet young grass, upon the carpet of the gods that
guard as I sleep, dreaming of my fortune amid this
garden of delight.

Now the dark descends but I am not afraid as the
spirits roam, they are the good who remain loyal
to the land, they are the brave who will remain
forever true, until the dawn - until the
end of time.

Roger Sharpe

To My Love

Let me begin the day looking into your eyes
And opening my being unto you;
Show me understanding, be loving and forgiving,
Stay within my heart and in everything I do.
In you I live and have my very being,
Feel deepest joy again
In the midst of deepest pain;
Make music out of misery -
And a song out of sorrow,
Cut me free from all that binds me -
Promise me tomorrow ...

Peggy Smallman

Empty Tomb

Amongst the endless falling waves of tarnished dying,
That in the pathways and soiled borders
Of this park find a shore,
And cut sharp against a sky crimson drown,
A stone, of remembrance,
Of youth, of War, of death, And yet,
Only they seem to remember,
Who cannot so easily forget.

I watched as the sky burst,
And ran with a stain that raped the evening of its form,
And I thought of those young men who died,
Of the Women who died
Of the children who died
Of the widows,
Of the maimed and crippled,
Of the mentally crippled
All forgotten by this great nation, this other Eden,
By my people, - by myself.

How could they not be left, but to gaze with bitter eyes,
These young men who just had to die, And Why;
Why because of War,
A Wave that cannot find its shore.

P A Stone

Catatonia

You bring body and soul into this church
With honest faces of duty
Thrown down like dice into a tigers' pit
I'm all sixes and sevens
Latin words of gobbledygook
Spooky, jumpstart crocodile clips
Snapping, snapping

You anoint my temples
There is no need to fear you
You can do me no harm
You bring me where I will be brought at last
The dark, the black; the familiar earth
Groaning, sodden, inner voices
Fall like life through my fingers

Each grasp clinches roots of hair
Commands these puppet strings
The pin shaved nerves of splintered lightning
To jig, to jar, to jolt
A scorpion filled mouth hisses
Its' malice pincered tongues
Thundering the mind with rumour

Scorched mystic fires alight beneath the surface
Of a body scarce half made up
Its' hyaline ebbs and flows, ebbs and flows
To a kindling conclusion
Chop-chop, chop-chop
You're all over now
Prophet: Where is the calm?

Vittoria Vaughan

Untitled

Some nights
'I' awake
With no point of reference
I don't recognise
The room
The objects
The time
The woman
'Myself'

A part of the Soul
Normally hidden
Becomes clear
Separated from the Whole
One night
'I'll' take a long walk
Away from remembering
Who 'I' am
'I'll' return forever
To
No point of reference

Mark Gott

No!

The sun is blood upon the hill,
The grass is brown,
The earth is still.
No breath of air
No bird in flight
No jumping frog
No cloud in sight.
The ground is sand
beneath my feet,
While all around me are asleep.
No water now, no brimming cup,
what will it take to wake them up!
No more the crests of waves to ride.
No dams required to stem the tide,
They are but bastions
on a barren country side.
The sun is blood upon the hill,
The land is dead,
The earth is still.

Constance Roper

Country Walk

Country walk
Was my teen years pilgrimage.
Romance feeling, rambling,
Meandering, partly in meditation
On lanes leading to diverse destination.
Exploring the hitherto unexplored.
Mind cultivating
My new green acres.
Every Sunday: Every Season,
Youth seeking
Something unspecified.
Finding
Village lights awaiting
Afternoon's late arrival
At lane's end.
More lights on less lanes now.
Country walk becomes suburban.
Original destination
Still unspecified.

Aubrey Bush

New Pyjamas for Hospital

Fresh from the crisp M & S bag
they will hold the smell of shops
for all of a day. You will wear them in
eventually, and meanwhile
they are virginal, no personality
and I shall hardly know you.
Alone, surrounded by Hospital
noises of trolleys and joking,
and the multiple shared discomfort,
you will not want the food
that was somebody else's order.

You left me the old blue pyjamas
with the button off, and the patch
and the threadbare bit by the pocket,
the out-of-date collar. I hug
their familiar softness at night,
imagine your shoulder, and miss
your warmth and your regular breathing;
the particular smell of your skin,
your hair, and the back of your neck.

Hilary Shields

We Come in Peace

Shattered limbs, lying alongside hazy dreams,
Wrapped snugly in the ideals of his own patriotism,
No words of anger does he utter,
Only a blood soaked groan of fulfilment.
His blood eventually uniting with the hard baked earth,
Soil and blood a returning of two brothers.
Slowly his body returns to that which made him,
Mother earth tenderly embracing her lost son.
And overheard the artillery barks, in a noisy epitaph,
The dark sky, saluting another valiant warrior.
Whilst onward moving the great army rolls,
Never having any time to stop,
They haven't even got time to die.
For they march in honour of their country,
And with every step they propel us nearer,
To a blissful Armageddon.
Bloated, fat men sitting behind closed doors,
Accountable for all,
They justify the death of man,
Behind the facade of a greater cause.
And mankind in a sad stupidity,
Nods its head in understanding.
Then in bout of vicious audacity, they call this cause peace.
But please don't cry for these poor soldiers,
Because they now hold a place in our colourful history.
If you must weep, cry only for yourself,
For you are the ones still living.

Steven McLuckie

Road Works on the M6

Wind from the east, the beasts
Are silent.
Moving across the landscape;
How can they escape
The endless conveyor belt?

Juggernauts, cars, caravans, naught
Between them.
Coaches, faces in the windows, where to?
Silvered heads forward
Towards journey's end.

Nose-to-tail, traffic halted,
Undaunted;
Ferry fast, home speed, swift delivery
Queue up to be off, hastening
To their next full stop.

The meadow bullocks stare;
No cares.
No desire to hurry, why worry?
A whole life's year ahead.

Roland Astall

Homecoming

Lowering skies, and twilight falling early.
After the frantic, feverish hurly-burly
Of the town, the air strikes dank and chill.
A mist writhes, soundless, rising from the fields,
A little wind disturbs the grass, and yields
Only a whisper, then is still.
My football echoes faintly in the lane.
I round a bend, it wanders on again,
No friendly traveller anywhere in sight.
Emerging from a wood a vixen prowls,
And distantly the haunting cry of owls,
Heralds the advancing night.

I shiver. Not with cold, but apprehension.
The brain, too quick, too ready with invention
Conjures up on all sides night's grim hosts.
Faces peer and leer from gnarled oak bough,
The whirling, swirling mist is peopled now
A conference of faceless ghosts.

Longing for the journey to be done,
I break into a jerky stumbling run,
Pulses racing, senses taut and strained.
Eyes peering through the swiftly deepening gloom
For first glimpse of a lighted cottage room,
the glowing proof of home re-gained.

At last it shows! Beyond the ash tree there.
Warm, welcoming, a mellow, yellow square.
Relief puts all my fears to flight.
Turning now the door knobs friendly dome,
Drinking in the joys of being home.
Shutting out the hostile night.

Dora Judson

The Gift

Gentle as the snow that falls,
my love for you.
Perfect as a blackbirds call,
sweet and true.
Deep and endless as the sea,
my love for you.
Strong and sturdy as a tree,
in glorious hue.
For all eternity and yours to keep,
my love for you.
Yours and yours alone to reap.
Forever new.
Shining constant as the stars above,
I give to you... my love.

Anne Harris

The Venom of the Adder

What news headlines flare for men who die like sheep?
Which reporters would bow their heads and weep?
There is only the lonely vigil of isolated guard huts,
The distant thunder of hidden bombs.
A single sullen thud suddenly puts
A deathly hush over rainswept tombs,
While mothers at home cry
In case their sons should die.

The innocent lie among the convicted
As still as any other.
The streets are lined with the evicted
From homes destroyed by a brother.
And still the fighting forges
Furrows of hate through the land,
Forming impassable gorges
Cast by the assassins hand.
The scars scale the longest ladder
And are strewn from border to border,
And like the venom of the adder
They destroy all sense of order.
And so, as is always the case,
Behind hate, man hides his face.

R J Maxwell

Nightfall

Beware the shadows of the night
Where hooting owls and black bats fly,
The silver moon hangs motionless
High in the diamond studded sky.

The badger ventures from her set
Her children play no fear of foe
And foxes hunt the countryside
Beware the sheep and baby doe.

When night is over daylight dawns
Through fields that whisper in the breeze
The animals hide and sleep all day
In safety deep within the trees.

Julie Gage

The Reluctant Bride

Not so fast
My life's still full
I'm not quite ready
To go a courting
With silent gentlemen
All dressed in black
It's not that I'm ungrateful
But I thought my first
Would be
More dashing

The satisfaction
In outliving all others
Is that you decide
What's right for you
And not
Great Grandad Puddlewick
Who used to preach the sermon
In the chapel
(But thinking of
The Dog and Duck)

But here I am
All set to meet
Not my maker
But Great Aunt Ivy
Who bless her
Dear Heart
Will still not know whether
To commiserate or congratulate
On my
Unmarried state

Ian Dannatt

The Student's Union Block

Her mouth moved her eyes were glazed
As she watched the moving screen.

Government scientists have taken samples for...

Through the taste of the stale smoke and beer
The clock on the wall was having a silent doze.

Suddenly she moves carrying her crisps as she goes.
Her mouth moved her eyes were dazed
As she peered at the bright red notice-board.

Succulent Strawberry Yogurt...

Was it the notice that said, 'Fight student poverty'
Or was it the ad. for the party, she heard in her head.

More than a hundred people were injured...
And the noise of the shop-till pinged.

Now back to her chair she moves
Her mouth now still, but her eyes still dazed
As she looks in silence at the screen.
Her sad face lights as a figure approaches
And his voice on her spell encroaches.

A Government spokesman said today...

The TV was on but the girl hadn't seen
The world, it's images corrupt and obscene.

A B Jamison

A Future Hope

Our world today is racked and riven,
With trouble and strife on every side.
And nations would rather sin and slay
Than in the Lord abide.
No wonder then, we pray and pray
For hope in the future years.
But we see a vision of sweat and strain
Through the salting tang of tears.
O God, in our hour of need of Thee
We ask Thy aid to find
A way to end this suffering,
The path of peace for mankind.
That one day, brother to brother will come,
No matter what colour or creed,
With hands clasped together in friendship
To look to the Lord for the lead.
Then the world will at last be united
God's Kingdom be nearer at hand
And the nations will travel together -
Led by Him to their own 'Promised Land'.

Enid Rathbone

Fond Memories

When I was young, many moons ago
I'd sit on my fathers knee
And listen quite enraptured
To the tales he told to me.
I'm not quite sure if all he told
Was the honest truth, and yet
I still remember all of them
I never will forget,
He'd tell of far off places
Lands across the sea
Swaying palms and dusky maidens
Geisha girls and scented tea
Thirsty trecks across the desert
Sleeping under the stars on summer nights
Listening to the roar of lions
Or over to Paris seeing the sights
Oh, if only I could have been there
And made those journeys with him too
Think of all the marvellous tales
That I would tell to you
So gather round my little children
Rest your heads upon my knee
And let me tell you all the tales
The ones my father told to me.

Roslyn Blyth

The Invisible Cell

The invisible cell that blinds your mind, full of emptiness
locking out all those who would be kind - and in it a mind
defying all rational thinking
Irrational mind - afloat in a mire, but gradually sinking.

'Snap out, snap out' - who shouts there?
Keep away and leave me in my lake of despair - ruing the day when
I was conceived - to be born into this purgatory where all are
deceived -
Into believing - in what? That which we are not?

A moment of solitude in my cell so large yet so small, the key, so
illusive
and yet - only I can see
The lock in which to turn the key to set me free and get back to my
path of destiny.

S Dellicompagni

Untitled

Shades of transparent whiteness draw their blinds
In succession confusing subconscious minds
Whilst cruel time with sculp and scalpel grinds
Decay at whim and fancy.
All life it finds.

Hushed beyond silence except for unhurried tread
Along obedient gangways, bordering each bed
Allowing passage of those who raise a spread
Above throat, lip and eyebrow
Eventually the head.

Are there footsteps the living do not hear
Which tell of an inevitable tide drawing near
Thus resignation dims awareness culling fear
Of immortality
And will I join you dear.

A Johnson

To a Chaser of Moonbeams

Chasing moonbeams seems to me, a pretty hopeless task.
To keep the things I cherish most, is all I ever ask.
To meet your eyes with mine, and in a glance to know and feel,
that time may pass and seasons change, but still our love is real.
Then as they meet, to feel our love fall round us like a shawl,
Within its bounds, a trespasser could find no place at all.
Enclosing precious memories, of laughter, love, and tears,
of fun, and peace, and tenderness, and sharing secret fears.
And from all this, a closeness, grown from time and loving care,
Just knowing quiet happiness, as long as you are there.
My senses swim, your eyes hold mine, their message clear to see,
and warmed by love, I turn away, my eyes and heart to free.
For just two people, time's stood still, and though no words have passed,

we've said, 'This love could never die,'
And this is all I ask.

Gloria Rough

The Old Church

I came upon it quite by chance
the old church on the hill,
No congregation worshipped there
Its organ now was stilled.

I thought about the caring hands
Who build this church with love
And all who did once worship
In this, now neglected house of God.

Its old door was open
I wandered in to pray
A shaft of light lit up the cross
I know that God was there.

C Hayes

Big Knives

What I need right now
Is stability, to feel safe
All around my space
Lies fear and confusion
Wrapped from head to toe
In glorious colours
These insecure colours won't leave me now
They cling so tightly, they hold so dear
I've shared my problems, held out my hand
To friends, I hoped for more
Than they could give
Trust was gone, speculation rose through
Contrived conversation, consequently
Out came the big knifes
Nothing like a big knife
For that warm sensuous feeling of security
Yes I do have problems
With my circle of fang faced friends
All ready and waiting, eyes bulging
For those fatal, misplaced words
Oh don't I live dangerous, to the edge
All my friends have now left
And here I am all alone
Sat in the dark, hoping someone will phone

Stephen Scott

Heron

Motionless,
Intent,
Frigid gaze piercing the water.
Only a few feathers flutter,
Stirred by the imperceptible breeze.
Frozen in stillness,
Statuesque,
As if its Gorgon stare reflected
Had turned it instantly to stone.

The intense gaze anticipates a fish below,
The spear hurls forward -
The fish is snatched from life,
Knowing nothing but the cataclysmic collapse
Of the roof of its world.

The hunter moves on
With long, halting, steps.

Richard Fraser

Any Sunday Afternoon

In the corner, not quite
holding our attention,
desperate men tunnel under wire.

Any Sunday afternoon is when we
dust down those escape plans
most of us cowards have shelved

but would we tunnel into
a chaos of freedom, to turn
and press an envious face against the glass,

forcing entry back into
the fathomable clutter of our lives;
institutionalised at last?

Boxed between cat and curtains,
two escapees shot, one battling on
towards an unknown frontier.

Julie Lumsden

Autumn Imagery

Have you looked at the wood in Autumn,
undressed of Summer spread?
Skeletal oaks and ashes,
their leaves dyed rustic red.
Clinging forlornly to the branches,
in patchy clumps of gold.
Features of the year turned from lemon-fresh to old.
Crispy, dry and crinkly, that crunches under foot
and crumbles into dust, at finger's slightest touch.
Delicately fragile, almost washed away,
the russet browns and crimsons, etched 'gainst a sky of grey.

Susan Allen

A Man Alone

The tests had been made, the verdict given
The good doctor had shaken his head,
Somewhere in his words he had mentioned six months
But the words hadn't reached to the bed.

That the Reaper should send such a message
Was not in the scheme of things,
Here were friends; the remains of a breakfast,
Mundane talk which the visitor brings.

And here he was, clutching a blanket
And any old straw that came by,
And the words that had proved too big for his ears
Were telling him still he must die.

A minute ago he had just been ill
Now his brain was reduced to a stare,
He looked round the room for a smile of reprieve
But found there was nobody there.

The coffin is pine and the handles shine
Reflecting the siliconed floor,
And the pews and the lectern as thick with wax
As the names of the men lost in war.

And after internment the house echoes loud
To the old ones, back from the brink.
The lion has killed, so the herd are at rest
And there's plenty of tea to drink.

Les Williamson

What's in a Name?

A lady from Sutton, Miss Cholmondeley,
Who was virtuous, modest and comely,
Loved a young chap from Blidworth, Jack Belvoir,
Who vowed that he'd never deceive 'er.

But a bounder from Warsop, called Wemyss,
'Ticed the good woman off, so it seems,
With the aid of a cad, name of Beauchamp,
To a spot where nobody could reach 'em.

When a gamekeeper bold, Henry Strachan,
Spied them struggling out in the corn,
He ran with his lad, Billy Gower,
And punched wicked Wemyss on the jaw.

Whereupon Miss C covered her charms,
Then went home with Constable Glamis,
And next day in marriage was given
By her guardian, good doctor Ruthven.

Bridesmaids were the two misses Myerscough;
Now, there's something I should like to ask you.
Would you mock at this tale with it's harsh pranks?
Just be thankful your name isn't Marjoribanks.

A J Dixon

Assassination of a King

He stands proud, dominant,
red breast on show,
jumps at the wire and gracefully opens his throat,

The summer rays beat down when he drew his last breath,
Killed out of love and lust by his delicate queen,
Stabbed and stabbed then left to die,

Cold, motionless as the ground,
eyes lost, proud feathers gone,
while all around the other birds shout to show the king is dead!

James Heald

Second Fiddle

The back of the queue is my usual place,
I'm never the one in the lead.
That I should be just a supporter
Some superior force has decreed.

We're all in our fishnets and spangles,
And lit by the spotlight's bright glow.
I'm kicking away in the chorus,
But I long to be star of the show.

I don't demand fame or a fortune,
But only to have some true worth.
To feel that it really does matter
If I do or don't stay on this earth.

I'm not such a total disaster,
Although it would seem I can't win.
So why must I play second fiddle.
When I want to be first violin?

Jean Hick

Wedding

You know this thing will never last
Against the test they say time sets,
For people come and go so fast
That all they've time for are regrets.
The assumption of a wedding ring -
A partner purchased with a kiss -
Belies the truth long years will bring;
That nothing stays the same as this.

And when you're young it seems so strange
That passion gets replaced by trust.
The aching hours that rearrange
The lost ingredients of lust.
For behind the din of wedding bells
Is the joyless ring of lawyers' tills.

Jan Coverley

Sunset

My mind so wordless,
That beauty should enshrine
The end of land.
Where fringed waves lap
The ragged rocks.
A fiery ball; energy waning
After the midday glare.
Reflections on cooler waters.
The artists dream
Sinking beyond. The horizon
Ablaze, with natures glory.
Sinking still deeper,
Gone.
A glowing stillness
Across the dark face of the water.

Barbara Surfleet

Thwarted Ambition
(Reflections on Bonfire Night)

You cannot catch the stars
As they spew into the night,
Etching earthly dreams
Onto eternal skies.
You cannot feed the fire,
Explosive force of flame -
Cannot prolong fleeting thought
Nor shield yourself from pain.
Briefly, as they shoot apart,
Blaze, and flash, and fall,
Dazzled by false brightness,
You will try to snare them all, yet
You cannot catch the stars
As they splutter to the ground.
See how fast they disappear -
Foiling outstretched hands.

Janette Sykes

Change of Mood

Powerfully, majestic breakers batter the torn rock,
Pounding, thrashing and bullying in their onslaught,
Flooding back and dwindling away
As if accumulating energy and breath for the next assault.
With fierce and furious rhythm, wave after angry wave
Crushes and tramples all that dare oppose it,
Like some grand army of the days of yore,
Its snorting steeds spurred on in frenzy,
Thundering madly, rank upon serried rank,
Hurling itself relentlessly, bent on complete destruction.

In calm tranquillity, the shimmering ripples lap upon the shore,
The fury of their earlier mood forgotten.
Spent is the anger and the show of strength
And in its place this lazy, happy peace holds sway,
Calm as the rippling grass upon the plain,
The tempest over and the battle done.

Jessie Wade

Reef to Wreath

So here I lie, my final resting place
Forever to remain in my white rock heartland;
A hewn off chunk, rough and ready,
Uniform pale grey and made for the job;
A lasting memorial for me and my many compatriots,
A criss-crossed signature for mile after mile;
Chalked lines on landscape, an inscription on a sward of green
But disregarded with ease, except by those who exclaim,
'Dry stone walling, there's a forgotten art.'
'It's part of our heritage like.'
Or the Summer stream of booted hikers
Crossing our boundaries via sole-smoothed stiles,
Then leave us, forever onwards.
Or geologists, for whom I'm a Latin name like Lithostrotion,
Those who would interrogate my innermost secrets.
How old are you?
What was your habitat?
Why choose an English National Park as your final resting place?
What was the nature of the waters that washed you,
caressed you, fed you?
Tell me of their temperature, clarity, salinity.
Oh yes! Those waters.
Bathed in tropical warmth, cocooned as by a lagged cylinder
In brilliant azure amidst rainbow fish darts.
A kaleidoscopic companionship of dancing light
Swirling and streaming in a flow of incessant liquidity;
Rich colours in a spectral bombardment.
But these are days of grey rain. My reef is now beached,
A haven for hikers, a shelter for sheep.

John M Carruthers

Cuckoo

You work by deception,
Bright eyes lurking in the leaves' green dark.
A long-tailed ghost intent
Upon that brief unguarded moment then, sly
The soft flight to another's nest.

Inside the egg your body's hireling learns patience.
A killer by remote control,
His brain's jelly sucks in heat -
The vital nerves are bending to your will.

Like Trojan fools these hosts will shelter him,
Bring meat as gifts.
You planned the ruse,
The Greek in him will do the rest.

David Peggs

Christmas Stuffing

We stuff our bags for Christmas
Buy all the goodies we can find.
We stuff the kiddies stockings full
We stuff the bird's behind.
We stuff the tills with money
'Til they're bursting at the seams
We stuff our faces 'till we're sick
With nuts and chocolate creams.
We stuff our minds with drivel
We are shown upon TV
The churches we leave empty -
Stuff Nativity.

Sally Wildman

Landlocked

Wolverhampton
(Thirteen letters)
You were certainly unlucky for me.
Confusing you
With Southampton,
I'd thought you were by the sea.

The coastal promise of Sandwell
Further led me astray,
But if you stand on the steps
Of Bilston town hall
You can't get much further away.

Diane Kaylor

The Last Flower

A rose gleams through the autumn morn.,
Shining and gleaming beyond the gloom.
Gold tinged with red; stippled with dew,
Mirror of dawn as the sun breaks through.

Carpet of brown and red, leaves on the ground.
Echoing shades of a summer long gone.
Skeletal branches, stark against clouds,
Cold with the promise of snows still to come.

Too late in the year, this sad, lonely bloom.
No more than a bud, beyond natures call.
It's lot is not to mature or grow old,
But lighten this landscape of dark decay.

This fleeting glory cannot be stayed.
Too soon colours dim to lustreless hues.
It's purpose ended, it fades fast away.
Leaving a memory of life unfulfilled.

Norman Brookes

Sweetly Your Smile (For Judi)

Sweetly your smile
Lingers in the air,
And your fallen hair
Clings to my clothes,
As I stare
At burning thoughts
Which are only shadows
Of a few hours ago,
And cry in the cold dark
Because you had to go.

So, I'll keep awake to-night,
All night,
And turn my eyes
Away from my marble bed
Which waits patiently
In the corner,
Like a monolith
With a grey indifference,
In a frost caught
Morning light.

G R Soppet

Boy on the Ledge

Boy on the ledge
not coming down,
from brick to drainpipe
clambering
out to see what's there
a bottle is found
in the roof of all places
attempts to come back
but to no avail
stuck, and the way is
down
into the marsh
into the stench
the journey has ended
and a smile has been found.

Mark Hudson

Land Reclamation

Grass tunnel, sliced, now bare.
Wind funnelled stirs a hair
On the matted flank of running splendour,
Thudding hooves of forelegs slender,
Sending rabbits to their holes
In the boles of dying alders.

Warped, unsightly rocky outcrops,
Stubborn to man's taming hand, mock
'Whitewashed' walls of shapely stones
Here are England's real bones!
Rising now to spurn the tractor,
Rid the fields of improved grassland.

No more Ministry grants for vandals,
Eating England from the handles
Of bright machines designed to mangle,
Crush and bury, and to strangle,
Meadow cranesbill, yellow cowslips,
Upland grasses, unruly brambles.

Ian J Forrest

A Sonnet to my Partner in Middle Age

So, middle-aged, on holiday, we climb
From beach to cobbled street of seaside town;
At ease we are and have no thought for time;
We shop and talk and watch the sun go down.

We hear the childish games like castanets
Click crisp and clear in park and village green
And watch dark, salty men tease fishing nets
While frothy ripples lick our toes numb clean.

But in the castle ruins we sense the threat
From crumbled monuments of stone, that meet
The passer's eye and cast a shadow long
And dark, for there we two do not belong:

As the world we see can only know decay,
So the love we feel grows younger day by day.

Peter Francis

Daffodil Bride

When the golden pathways spread,
Interlaced by lissom trees,
Then's the time when she will wed,
With spring's own smile for memories.

The thrush will wake her, sharp and keen,
In the faint light frost at dawn,
Small feathered ecstasies unseen
Call joy upon her bridal morn.

The happy bells across the hills
Will chime their call for all to meet,
Will echo in the daffodils
That swing and sway, the bride to greet.

A blossom fair herself, is she,
Her sunlit hair, her radiant face.
Pray blessings on her; None can be
More worthy of the words of grace.

May golden pathways span her days,
Shadowed with but few regrets;
May she find the unknown ways
Sweet as springtime violets.

Elsie Cawser

An Enquiry

Where are the poets of Africa,
Now that the Empire is dead?
When will the flowering talents
Suddenly come to a head?

There are swimmers and hurdlers
And marathon runners,
Politicians and boxers and
Artillery gunners.
But where are the men with the pen?

When will some bard of the Cameroons
Publish some witty lampoons?
Or a subject of Seretse Khama
Write a drama.

They've changed all the names
Of the continent's cities,
But where are the new Afro-ditties?

Is there nowhere in print
A Somali Peer Gynt?
Or stanzas on life that are thrilling.
Is there nothing to add,
Be it good or it bad,
To Buchan and Haggard and Kipling?

Where are the poets of Africa
Now that the Empire is dead?
When will the blossoming talents
Suddenly come to a head?

Bernard Ryan

The Fix

After the Fix of two Fortunes
Crossed in the dirt
Only the heart - and the heart only
Hears - the music of the Word
Unheard, by human ears

Only the face - and the face only
Fears, the surface - of the lake
Of the dream - unknown
Unspoken but grown
In the shape of human hands

And across the barren land
Came a creature - dying of thirst
Crawling between - Heaven and Earth
Down to the lake
To the water where
The water waits...

Untouched, as the years tick by
Reflecting the earth
Reflecting the sky
And washing the bones
(on the stones of the shore)
Of an ancient creature

Who crawled between - Heaven and Earth
And died of thirst
Unable to Face - his own Face
Down in the water
Of the deepest lake.

Mark Gwynne Jones

Seal Coats

The seals entrails
Left red trails
In the white snow
While man maintains
He went to great pains
For his unjustly gains.

Grace McKie

Eternality

The people of the Hawk came from the West.
They laid lands bare, ravaged crops,
Doing everything history would expect from them,
Crime carriers doomed to damage order
And pass on, almost unnoticed in time,

Thunder from their setting sun, carnage
Crazed, they razed an ancient, ageing culture
Clean as a picked bone, and not a stone
Of temple outstayed then, though gods
In vengeance levelled then to dust.

The people of the Snake came from the East.
Fang against talon clashed, blind worm
Spread hood above the bloodied bird and bit,
Quick, and death dulled the disenchanted eye
And stone framed the hard cold act of iron.

Bestaries of people, all confidently
Emblemed will blossom in blood-time or peace
Until the world's-end, Beneath that final sun
Sword and plough will shape as ring, as one,
And bone, bestoned, shall sing the last word.

Neil Barks

Metamorphosis

Heat hit the stone
till temper dripped
from less crude planes
and brazen bends
sprang up in maiden skin.
Shimmering scales grew
and twisted
until the fine lass
hissed and wound
and slowly found
the other face.

Alas!
The day cracked
and fright poured
from scorched clouds
and drenched the serpent
until the clinging blades
revealed a lily.

Helga Tallon

Arizona Skies

Night black at its deepest,
Dawn holds its breath.
Then red pinks the edges of the distant hills
As the sun creeps upwards and the day desert wakes.
Morning bursts into life
And for an instant - a moment of brilliance -
The sky aches white.
Dazzling, blinding, new.
Red streaks back -
Long tentative fingers trailing across the expanse of sky,
They merge and swamp all else
Until blue arches triumphant
And the world moves on.

Later - late in the afternoon -
Coolness heralds the sunset.
Red stakes a fresh claim
On the vast acres of near cloudless air
Dotting, then striping, then pouring
Its dye on the sky,
Fighting off impending night.
A tiny solo white cloud lightens briefly
Before losing the one-sided battle.
Red sweeps across from desert to mountain
As if unaware of the blackness of night
Ascending behind it.
An instant. It is gone.
Beaten again red must always lose.
Black celebrates briefly
Before giving way to sparkles of white
As the stars spangle the sky like a banner.

D G Collins

Absent Friends

Time... time...
ticks... tocks... and
locks together
minute bits of people.
Fragments of our hearts,
attached
yet some
detatched.

A face in a crowd, smiles, glows
and you know
warmth oozes from it.
Melting into other's pores.
Not yours.
So bitter sweet.

Tick... tick...
click.
Fate deals you a heart.
A friendship starts
as you look back.

In time...

Timothy Whawell

Today I Lost

Today I lost my sense of humour,
I keep it in a jar marked
'Sense of Humour'
On the kitchen shelf
Next to the confetti
And dead Father Christmas's.
I got it out this morning,
I always take it shopping
It helps me to cope with inflation
And it usually finds some incident to feed on
You will get fat I tell it.
I left it playing in the garden with the dog,
Whilst I found the shopping paraphernalia.
The dog came in when I called, he likes the biscuits
I give him as a bribe.
I cannot bribe my sense of humour,
It jumped over the wall
With a chuckle
And was gone.
It was not a good day without it.
I didn't laugh when I broke the eggs,
Burnt the potatoes and tore my skirt.
This evening when out for a walk with the dog
I found my sense of humour
In a field of cows and buttercups
Exhausted
And dirty.
I picked it up washed it in a puddle,
Put it in my pocket, and went home smiling.

Ursula Gratton

Race

I wish you had not said you loved me
and fallen limp, prone before me;
now I cannot catch you up
and will never seem to care as much.

Too easy to make a simple mistake,
to say you felt the love I'd faked;
too easy to smile and surrender it all
to a heart too small, if there at all.

In our race to fall in love,
you came first
so I gave up.

Neil Clarke

Forgotten Friends

We languish in a garret of dark silence,
Accepting each layer of dust
As a blanket of sad neglect.
Perhaps a fate unjust
When viewed in the light of their former respect for us.

Yes, we kept them happy,
Winter days of indoor discontent
We changed to mirth,
Each growing one of them went
To a soft pillow at even with our friendship and our worth.

But what of our value now?
Will they, below, some day ascend
With other girls and boys,
Our present dusty solitude to end,
And make a new alliance with old friends - we toys?

Gordon Smythe

From a Mother

Who's done this to my dear young babies
Who's done this to my grown-up men
Who once walked the floor towards me
Who once took three steps and fell

What's happened now to my smiling babies
What's happened now to my brave young men
Who once read the cornflakes packet
Who once counted one to ten

Where's the breath in my laughing babies
Where's the breath in my shouting men
Who once ran the fields of Lenton
Who once built a secret den

Why is there blood on my dear young babies
Why is there blood on my grown-up men
Who gave the orders to take them forever
And tore out the heart of a mother again.

Martin Wright

Love

Love is a time of enchantment
We are caught by its silken thread
Our dreams, our desires and our longings
Entangled within its web
While we're in love it's exciting
We float away on a cloud
We hear music in the silence
Alone in the midst of a crowd
To the young it's a time of magic
To the old it is comfort and care
For both it brings June and December
And all our days are fair
Charmed, bewitched and bewildered
Through the eyes of love we see
Wonders that never happen
A world that will never be
We say we'll be true forever
We swear by the stars above
Love is a time of enchantment
And how willing we are to love

L Barnett

Is That It

What is poetry ?
Is it enough
To space the words attractively,
Across the empty page?
Or,
To so balance the vowels
Consonants and aspirates
That the mere click
And hiss and rumble
Becomes a music of its own.
Or is the way the words fall
An indifference?
And only the meaning makes the poem.
Or is arrangement all -
The very coincidence
Confluence and conjunction
Of unlikely word and phrase
So artfully disposed as to arouse
Strange ideas
And thoughts
Hitherto unspeculate
Bubble up
And sing and simmer in the mind
Is that it?

J Archer

The Dreamer

The dreamer leaned back against the wall,
A smile spread across his happy face,
A paintbrush tilted in one hand.
A masterpiece he felt sure;
The hue of scarlet on the butterfly perfect
The ease of the trees stretching in the wind
All captured on canvas.
An idyllic picture of the world today.
He uses his artists licence.
He smiled to himself when he looked from the nuclear
Cluttered site, the dead bodies and the destruction,
And looked at his idyllic picture,
His ideal picture of the world.
And God shed a single tear.

Kelley Peeling

Chance Meeting

Three years have gone
Since I touched you -
Thoughts in an old man's pub
Where battered old cases
Enjoy the knock-off.
I drink too much
Perhaps deliberately
And, in daring, place a fingertip
On the back of your hand
To feel the skin of you.
And then a kiss comes
With seconds of intoxicated
Closed eyed dizziness.
I board the bus home
Despite alternatives
As, through glass, you
Promise a letter and
Mouth my address -
I hardly believe you remembered.

Denise Lee

The Menin Gate

Above the carnage and the mud
Would not the sun have shone
As it shines now on the Menin Gate
In golden October - a lifetime on
From the madness that my father knew?
Did he stand here transfixed
By an autumn sky as magical,
Unmindful of the shattered town
That was the Wipers of his youth?
And I, the unlikely scion,
Chanced by ten thousand metal deaths
That did not bear his name,
Can savour a Flanders set with mourning stones
Amidst pacific fields. The shining walls
Lean in, on every inch a name:
Ten thousand sons, whom chance would spare no seed,
My tears fall now for you.

Out in the bitter mud
Of Passchendaele
A blighty sent my father home
To his posterity.
Posterity made flesh
Enjoys the sun - and weeps.

D Hewett

Seasons

It came too soon
The month of June
When all is fresh and new and sweet
And lovers start to meet in parks
Exchange shy glances, warm embraces
The sun penetrating to their hot hearts.

I longed for October
The whole summer over
For sharpness of air and crispness of ground
The wind kidnapping the leaves, and for me
Refreshing the empty chambers of
My broken heart.

Beverley Cherry

Bewildered Owl

Mid elfin greenwood
A lonely elm tree stood,
Upon its bough
A feathered guest,
A bewildered owl
In a cuckoo's nest.

Gerald Aldred Judge

The Outcast

Garrotte the traitor
With a scream,
Battered travelling leather jew,
Nail my rawhide
To a tree
With your winklepickered shoe.

David Bishop

Le Petit Bonheur

Watching the pale sun rising across the morning sky,
Smelling the applewood burning, seeing the embers die.
Holding a new born baby, kissing its downy head,
Rememb'ring sleeping children, tucked up in their bed.
The web of life is woven from such loved threads as these,
No thread alone is strong enough to give a sorrow ease.
Together, they make a shelter to soften grief and pain.
You know that when tomorrow comes, you can face your life again
So store these joyous, happy days and when you're feeling sad,
Open the door marked Summer, remember and be glad.

Jean Askin

Industrial Wasteland

I walked the stoned and crumbling ruins
Here where clocks have stopped and all shifts ended
Through shafts of falling daylight
Cutting from the shattered panes
And through the sorry silence
Of iron muscle rusting
All power cut and drained
And oily patches of industrial blood
Made rainbow by the dripping rain
I stopped and listened into that silence
Where once the iron giants roared
Now only the sound of a tapping breeze
As it wonders through the unhinged doors
Combed by cut and dangling cable
Hissing through the vacant stores
Carrying whispers through the vaults
Like muttered prayers within cathedral walls
And how the silence cried out
For the vanished congregation
for all the hammering and sweat
That built and fuelled a nation
For times long dead
And the skill of men
Scattered by the four winds
Never to meet again
Here the bench of one mans labour
There the tools of anothers bread
Ghosted now by redundant labourers
Who left the sleeping giants for dead.

Ryszard Napierski

Michael

His mind was broken
Long before his body;
Many before me
Knew this.
And on the day
It seemed an effort
Even for the clergy
To say the words
That betrayed anything
Good
Within him.
But his was the only shadow
To fall near to me
When once I came so low.
Now his escape
Is complete
Before anyone chanced
To reach out
And touch
A deceptive kind
Of humanity
Just hard to understand.

Barry Taylor

War Relief

Bullets whistled through the air.
Shells were dropping everywhere.
The air was thick with cordite stench.
The soldier huddled in his trench.
Not a coward but much afraid.
As the battle raged he knelt and prayed.
Then he felt a sickening stomach pain.
And he shouted out in fear.
Down his leg oozed a liquid stain
He felt that death was near.
His comrade rushed up to his side.
as he heard that anguished call.
The soldier just felt numb and cried
'Now I feel no pain at all.'
He touched his leg and said a prayer
His fingers were sticky and hot.
He said as he held them in the air.
'If my fingers are red I'm shot.'
His comrade said, 'They are not red,
They are a mucky brown.'
In shame the soldier hung his head
For he'd let his regiment down.
He'd got no wound to brag about.
Just the memory of a natural mishap.
But it proved to him without a doubt
That war was a load of crap.

J Inger

Pilgrimage to the Pier

A gentle soul absorbed in dreams
He trudged along the pier,
Sad heart enthralled as he recalled
The times they'd lingered here.

How many grief tinged summers fled
Since that final trip was made;
He could see her now so pale of brow,
As she watched the crowds parade.

Cavorting children twisted past
And increased his since of loss.
Ecstatic cries neath summer skies
As they clutched their candyfloss.

Withered ladies clothed in grey,
Oblivious to his pain,
In girlhood dear may have trod this pier
During old Victoria's reign.

He rested on a pale green seat,
Heard murmurs from the sea,
Gulls wheeled high and screeching by
Disturbed his reverie.

He produced the precious photograph,
Her soulful eyes shone clear,
As to old dreams dead he fondly said
We have come back then dear.

R B Lister

Harvesters of the Night

Blind purses of leather
Hung from rafters
In warm roof spaces,
Above shattered shells
                    and discarded wing cases,
Clutched in the senseless,
Summery night,
By sorting invalids,
                    in finger-like flight.
With no scented touch,
Nor sighted line,
They reap night's bounty
                    so crunchingly fine.

David Denny

A Gentle Stillness

The light breeze rustles
In the tall beech tree,
As the waxing moon
Shimmers palely through the
Gathering, rolling, night cloud,
My heart is full. It suddenly lurches,
Then aches, with a mixture of joy and a
Sadness, as I listen to the sound of a
Gentle Stillness.

Doreen Hewgill

On Being Alone

Being alone doesn't always mean
Being lonely.
In fact sometimes it's true
That loneliness is caused by mixing
With too many not too few.

Oneness with myself is time.
Time to think or dream
Or sit. Just sit and do nothing
Except perhaps to scheme
Within my head.

Thought's flow unhindered when
No sound is heard from others, or from things.
To savour when the night is mine
And no one else's.

Jean Heap

Approach of Spring

Bare the branches, harsh the hand
Of Winter as she scours the land,
Where once spring flowers gently grew
In shades of yellow, pink and blue.

Frost bedecked, the hedgerows face
The cutting wind's ice-cold embrace.
Forgotten now the Summer scene
Of sun-warmed meadow, lush and green.

Pond and fountain, ditch and dyke,
Freeze, picturesquely grotto-like,
As if has come with tip-toe tread
Paralysis and struck them dead.

Of living creatures, large and small
Some will survive and some will fall
Victim to Nature's chosen end
That none can change nor comprehend.

Then suddenly one day will see
The seasons change mysteriously.
The earth, expectant, breath indrawn,
Waits, anxiously, to be reborn.

And so the year rotates again
To neutralise the wrack and pain
Of winter, which in turn bears Spring
New life, new growth, new everything.

E Stormont

Fantastic Plastic

Too many people
Living plastic lives
With plastic husbands and
Plastic wives
With plastic kids and plastic cars
Drinking plastic drinks in plastic bars
Having plastic sex on a Saturday night
After turning off the plastic light
In case one of them might see
The plastic people they turned out to be.

Ron Stewart

Retford Market

The twice weekly open air
Market in the town Square
Is a piece of theatre
To which scene shifter and actor
Have brought a similar load
For years along the Great North Road.

Grimsby fish, Leicester cheese,
Sheffield knives, Nottingham lace,
Wheatley strawberries, Rampton beans,
Mansfield tights and Boston fruit:
The ancient names flow again
As they did from the Domesday pen.

Awnings belly and flap
Over nectarines from Sicily,
Brown rice from Surinam,
Salad from California,
Raisins from Afghanistan.
The world shrinks and Retford Square
Is a global everywhere.

Children finger a new toy,
Mothers back-to-school clothes;
Grandmothers watch the Town Hall clock
Swallow generations up.
Minor characters stop to chat
And catch up on the sub-plot,
Its entrances and exits.
The cast is always changing.

Yet scene, plot and characters all stay
For a performance another day.

Joan Board

The Trout

And in the river's deep, dark shining
I saw the beauty of his grace,
Slowly drifting through the willows
Within that sweet and shady place.
The gentle ripples fluted stillness
Touched his softly supple skin,
Shimmered slightly in the sunlight,
Found a freely flowing fin.
Lying in the dappled darkness,
Swimming slowly to and fro,
He majestically wanders
In the cool green river glow.

Elizabeth Welch

But Once a Year

It's time to go up in the loft again -
Take Christmas out of its box,
Dust off the record with carols,
Are the shepherds still watching their flocks?
Bring down the dusty old baubles
And the tinsel that's losing its shine,
Look! Here's the tree, good as ever -
With branches of real plastic pine.
Aah...the angel is losing his halo,
His robes and his wings are all creased,
Just an effigy sprinkled with glitter,
Was there really a star in the East?
Well... I've assembled these seasonal trinkets,
And the house looks festive again,
But somehow the magic is lacking -
Let's add a touch of good will to all men!

Betty Taylor

Hadfield - The Two of Us

The sky, cold eyes and aged cloud eyebrows,
Watches us.
'It's like an oil painting', you say;
But beyond it, I know, lies void.

They have torn the hills up
Like garden weeds,
And tossed them into history.
Crazy-paving housing estates
Cover the mess for the meantime.

Your loving eyes, blue as the wind,
Still see the hills and the summer.
I, though, see the bulldozers waking,
Lifting their scoops,
advancing.

Maurice Tattersdill

April Showers

Tom's taken off his long johns.
The weather's turned quite mild.
The April showers reminded him
Of when he was a child.
The adage said May flowers will come
and Spring itself be in full bloom.
Another adage he forgot
Regarding May's inconstant plot,
To catch the unwary; make them pay
For acting far too hastily,
By casting even a single clout
Before the month of May is out.

EPITAPH

To all you passers by, take note
And learn your Proverbs as by rote.
Follow the dictates which they give.
They may well help you longer live.

Tom Gibbons

Noosepaper

Read it
Yet do not receive it
With open arms
Or with great alarm
This forest of fiction
With its roots so deep in scandalous soil
These so called truths
That twist and coil
Tormenting your sanity and stealing your dignity
This tabloid of dirt
With its paper thin lies
And its mountain of falseness
From its press-gang spies
Ruined in print
So vivid and cruel
Thrown into the centre page drowning pool.

G Holt

My Little Room

Here I sit in my little room,
All is quiet, I am alone
The birds have sung,
The sun has shone,
Now it rains, for you have gone.

There is a feeling in the air,
Can it be that you are there,
Do you know, I despair
Do you know that I still care.

I can hear in the wind,
That ageing song that you would sing,
And the laughter it would bring,
Winter's here, gone is spring.

Sitting here I will remain,
And the song remains the same,
For who am I to lay the blame,
Life is life, so full of pain.

Robert Lamond (16)

Marilyn Monroe

You sang to the bottle,
through lips as red as wine.
Through your window
and your hourglass figure,
time was running out.
You touched many souls,
but yours remained twisted.
The natural beauty of a Goddess
clothed the sadness
of an inner emptiness.
You searched for safety,
for warmth and love,
but chemical tears
stained your soft skin
and self discontentment
raped your pained soul.
You needed love,
but spotlights created shadows
behind your silken body
and your hopes were hidden,
never to be fulfilled,
as your attractive charm
disguised the cries
of a lonely, confused dreamer.

Jolyon Oakes

Teardrop

The globule of sadness falls,
Precious, like a little gem,
Yet fragile. Delicate,
It glistens in the light,
A perfect work of art.
Swiftly, gently it falls,
Small, weak; touched it melts away.

C Greatorex

The Haggis

On Scottish hillsides long ago, the Haggis herds would graze.
Munching gorse and bracken on sunny summer days.
And every Scottish household had its own Haggis pet,
Ideal to wipe your boots with if the day should turn out wet.

But food supplies were getting scarce (there'd never been a lot)
And finally the household pet was put into the pot,
And though it tasted awful, and was difficult to carve,
They'd grit their teeth and swallow - it was either that or starve.

The problem with the Haggis is, it's very slow to breed.
Like pensioners and pandas, it seldom feels the need.
But scientists at Glasgow Zoo show in their last Prospectus
A plan to breed a randy kind, called 'Haggisii Erectus'.

But still the Haggis numbers have steadily declined,
And now in 1992, its very hard to find,
And what you see in butcher's shops is Haggis substitute,
A trick to fool the tourists (or at least the less astute).

It's something made from sheep's entrails, and Marmite meat extract
And someone ought to sue 'em, under t'Trade Descriptions Act.
So; if you're offered Haggis, particularly if you're foreign,
Politely answer 'Thankyou, no', or more rudely ' Up your Sporran!'

Fred Harrison

Should I?

I burdened you with silent hopes
-hopes you could not guess
I should have kept my dreams in check.
I should have wanted less.

I showed to you a hidden place,
-a place not shown before.
I should have numbed that inner ache.
I should have sealed that door.

I frightened you with too much need
-need I did not hide.
I should have shown a stronger face.
I should, my love, have lied.

I looked to you to show the way
-the way you knew, you said.
I should have taken up the lead
I should, my love, have led.

I trembled as your anger spilt
-spilt and left me broken.
I should have voiced the fear I felt.
I should, my love, have spoken.

So, I have not done what I should
Should I have been another?
Should I have acted differently
-or sought a different lover?

Wendy Morrison

The Study

India Ink. Lamplight. Dust.
Tobacco, stale and acrid on the tongue.
Leather chairs, soft and sagging,
Bottom shaped. Brightly-berried holly
Imprisoned in a vase. Mildewed
First editions crowd the walls.
Christmas cards astride a woollen rope,
Robins and rabbits and angels blowing horns.
In the hearth diseased logs of elm,
Spit sap, sickly sweet.

Upon the rug the faithful friend
Dreams of former glories on the windswept moor
And pheasant, warm and bloody in his mouth.
While at the desk his master, bent and grey,
Throws down his pen and watches discontentedly
As the world turns white beneath a mystical
Cloak framed in blood-red velvet. In the barn
A young man bled of hope as through an open vein
Finds warmth and comfort in a bed of hay
And weeps in thankfulness.

Joan Tomkinson

In Style

You pause from topping drinks and sit with us
One moment given to rest. That energy
Promises to swing the party on till dawn.
Your eyes are wet with wine and laughing friends;
Dark hair falls easy, and your feet drawn up
Fold limbs to captivate a camera's charm.

Now what you sit behind is one-way glass.
I turn its frame in search of date or town,
And sooner than tell you after all this while
What being confronted with you does, I'd send
Your image, secretly, and share your thought
That fringes and high hems are back in style.

Neil Croll

Lament

Where are the works to tell my grief?
And having the words, how can I know
Which stanza, verse or poem best
Would serve to heal my endless woe?

Where are the words to tell my loss?
And finding the words, how can I guess
Which tender cadences will fill
The void, or make it softly - less?

Where are the words to measure pain?
Or writing the words, which ones will calm
Or lend some surcease to the strife
Some solace, some annealing balm?

Where are the words to tell the death
Of most that made my life seem fair?
There are no words - there is no way!
One phrase is all - she is not there!

Gillian Beardow

Body Through the Looking Glass

The body
Before it sleeps
Sits, contemplates
The fluids and flakes of skin
Lost
Day after day.

There are hairs
Where they say there shouldn't be
Hairs-on our smooth women's skin
Creeping past the bikini line
Crowning our breasts
Invading our chins.

At times it's an animal
With pockets of smells
Some foul, some intriguing
Seductive.

Then a unique story is told
On each face,
Textured and pitted by the years
Eroded by the sweat
-tears.

To say nothing of the ideas
Hoarded inside
Spat out with saliva
Or swallowed.

Esme Zarins

Perceptions of Reality

The perceptions of reality we create
Depend on the our state of being
Depression see's the walls falling in
On a claustraphobic planet
Dreary days seem so vague
When in an ecstatic mood
The world has no bounds
Hot summer days
The sun smiling down
The smell of fresh new life
In the air
Summer is a truly wondrous time
When everyone is high on life
We all inhabit the same Earth
But we each live in our own world
Seeing things in a different light
Different realities.

Nik Aitchison

Distant Dreams

I seemed to see a distant world,
Where all mankind was one,
I seemed to see an end to war,
A never setting sun.

The leaves stayed green, the people young,
The days were long and full,
Of mirthful laughter, almost sung,
From faces never dull.

The blacks, the whites, the reds and blues,
The greens and pinks and yellows,
Looked all around saw things anew,
With eyes yet bright, still mellow.

I saw this in a distant dream,
Stopped by a nudging dawn,
But as a trickle to a stream,
It flows to those un-born.

Michael John Jackson

Thoughts From Wetton Hill

Perhaps the ancients knew well
That at this wild grand height,
Heaven is near.

How can you not feel the desire
To touch, taste, absorb velvet grass
As animals would?

Voluptuous, shapely hills, alive,
With sensuous textures
And evening mists.

Here would I bring a lover,
To meet a stronger master
And be humbled.

F Cork

The Elm

Like you I wait.
Like you, disease gnaws at my roots.
I stand alone and ugly
Waiting for a cure which can be found
Through waiting still.
Incapable, to do much more than
Waiting.

Like you I think.
My mind will be the last to go,
And leaving just my shadow
As a small reminder to the world
That I was here,
Where now this single shadow stands
Waiting.

Like you I laugh.
Like you I was a mockery
To those who would have loved me.
From those whom I sought love - rejection.
But now I find
That this is fading, as I am standing
Waiting.

Like you I watch.
Like you I see what others miss.
What fools they are, that love
And think through love they know the answer.
For that, I've always known,
But knowing makes it worse, when you are
Waiting.

Cathryn Lamble

A Close Encounter

Fear, electric, stunning, heart is pounding
Alarms in my brain are sounding
My whole body feeling-
pins and needles flowing through it
Then receding.

'Bloody idiot' says his voice beside me
Is he blind can't he see?
He's gone, we travel on
He passed in silence
Isolated in a world of his own
And yet my body shook
It was violence.

From my heart a deep sigh of peace
From fear I find release
Thank you God it didn't happen.

Margaret Topham

Rocks

I like to rub shoulders,
With Millstone Grit Boulders.
Rocks that are as old as,
The Derbyshire moors.

Proudly they stand,
Untouched by mans hand.
Upon that wild land,
Where a winter wind roars.

Beaten by weather,
Alone or together,
In peat or in heather,
So bare and so bleak.

Sculptured by wind and rain,
Long may they never wane,
For ever to remain,
The pride of the Peak.

K Ormiston

Love Poem

From heat of sun
From haggard moon.
I come
To the secret forest of
desire, alone, unarmed.

Each slender tree.
A hostile watchfulness,
Challenges the path of
Strangers feet.
Bending low only when
lovers hands stroke them.
Then at peace.

Enid Parkin